8 Rules of COMMUNICATION for SUCCESSFUL MARRIAGES

CHARACTER HEALTH.COM

By **Dr. Steve and Megan Scheibner**

EIGHT RULES OF COMMUNICATION FOR SUCCESSFUL MARRIAGES

By Dr. Stephen and Megan Scheibner
Copyright © 2016. All rights reserved.

All Scripture quotations, unless otherwise indicated, are taken from the New American Standard Bible Copyright © 1960, 1962, 1963, 1968, 1971, 1972, 1973, 1975, 1977 by the Lockman Foundation. Used by permission.

The use of material from various websites does not imply endorsement of those sites in their entirety.

No part of this publication may be reproduced, stored in a retrieval system, or transmitted in any form or by any means—electronic, mechani-cal, photocopy, recording, or otherwise—without the written permission of Megan Scheibner.

Produced and Distributed by:

Character Health Corporation
101 Casablanca Ct.
Cary, NC 27519

CharacterHealth.com

ISBN: 978-0-9963270-0-8

Printed in the United States

Rule 1
Learn to Listen 6

Rule 2
Find Out The Facts… 14

Rule 3
Think Before You Speak! 28

Rule 4
Don't Get Defensive! 38

Rule 5
Consider One Another's Spirit 46

Rule 6
Guard Your Tongue 54

Rule 7
Raise the Standards 62

Rule 8
Deal With Anger 68

Conclusion 76

Resources 87

EIGHT RULES OF COMMUNICATION FOR SUCCESSFUL MARRIAGES

BY STEVE & MEGAN SCHEIBNER

One of the best books we have ever read on the subject of communication between husbands and wives is _Love and Respect_ by Dr. Emerson Eggerichs. We've read a ton of books on marriage and relationships; what sets this book apart is that Dr. Eggerichs "gets it." His book should be a resource on every couple's bookshelves.

The importance of good communication cannot be overstated in marriage. In fact, good communication is absolutely vital to the overall health and quality of every type of relationship. Good communication may not come naturally, but it can be developed. The development of good communication can be a make-it or break-it proposition in your marriage. Conversely, poor communication will tear down walls of unity and build distance and bitterness in the marriage relationship. It often happens without us even thinking about it. Maybe we just say what's on our minds and tell it like it is. When this occurs, damage is inevitable, and we are caught wondering what just happened. Some people clam up or choose not to speak at all; this is another form of poor communication. Poor communication may be what comes naturally to us, but the wise husband or wife will do the hard work necessary to eliminate miscommunication and replace it with healthy, relationship-building models of affirming and encouraging communication.

Husband/Wife, Parent/Child, Employer/Employee, Pastor/Congregation, regardless of the type relationship, each will thrive or fail based on quality of the communication between the parties.

Dr. Eggerichs refers to "cracking the communication code" between husbands and wives, and although his book is aimed at improving marriages, the truths he shares could be applied to any intimate relationship. In fact, this book is a wonderful resource for those couples contemplating marriage. Beginning well, in the communications department, will circumvent many of the problems encountered in the first few months of marriage.

I (Steve) have worn many hats over the years, husband, father, Naval Officer, senior pastor, airline pilot, college professor, and most recently, corporation president. Regardless of the role I am playing, good communication can mean the difference between relational success and failure. Principles of good communication transcend relational boundaries. What is good for a marriage will be good in your business and community relationships as well. Allowing yourself to be lax in your home communications will most certainly spill over into your work and social relationships. With that in mind, let's look together at how we can break the "communication code."

We want to help you "crack the communication code" by devoting some time to exploring what we call the "Eight Rules of Communication for Successful Marriages." We have taught these eight communication tools for many years and to thousands of people. No one is exempt from the need to develop good communication skills, and no one has perfected this art. Every day brings new opportunities for growth and progress in our communication skills. Of course, every day affords us opportunities to "put it off until tomorrow" in regards to developing more effective communication skills. What will be the characterization of your day? Growth and improvement or stagnation and decay in the communication realm?

I (Steve) am a trained and experienced marriage counselor, who has counseled more than 500 couples in various states of disrepair over the years. Together, my wife and I have helped couples prepare for marriage, have encouraged couples as they fine-tune their marriage, and have worked with couples to rebuild a disintegrating marriage. I have been married to the fair and lovely Megan for 29 years. Although our relationship is not perfect (no one has a perfect marriage), I have learned a thing or two over the years about good communication from the most patient woman on the planet.

I have trained corporate executives, military officers and enlisted personnel, married couples, singles, men's groups, and youth all around the world. Regardless of the age, gender, or type of relationship, effective communication does not happen by mistake. Let us share with you some established guidelines that will improve communication and help you "crack the communication code."

"We want to help you crack the communication code by devoting some time to exploring what we call the Eight Rules of Communication for Successful Marriages."

-Steve & Megan

RULE 1

LEARN TO LISTEN

"Most people do not listen with the intent to understand; they listen with the intent to reply."

-Stephen R. Covey

The 7 Habits of Highly Effective People: Powerful Lessons in Personal Change

RULE 1

Learn to Listen

The Proverbs are didactic wisdom literature. Didactic means "to teach." A cursory look at the book of Proverbs will show you God's emphasis on the need to grow in wisdom, and then to utilize that newly acquired wisdom to build healthy and God-honoring habits for living.

In this age of endless input, we find ourselves drowning in a sea of information yet starving for wisdom.

Good and effective communication must have as its source wisdom. Good communication is not simply the mutual exchange of information between two or more people. It is much more than that! Good communication must emerge from a foundation of wisdom and core values. Wisdom and core convictions develop when we **learn to listen**.

Wisdom is developed as we spend time digging into God's Word, seeking God's direction in prayer, and searching out counsel from those with well-developed biblical character. Wisdom does not happen by accident! The development of wisdom takes time, commitment, and let's be honest, hard work. Gaining wisdom isn't a once and done proposition either. "I gained some wisdom today… Check that block." No, the acquisition of wisdom will be an ongoing proposition until we step from here to Glory. Our goal is to see you make that eternal transition with a legacy building reputation for God-honoring communication.

As we grow and develop wisdom, we will naturally desire to listen more effectively. Whether it is listening to the Word of God, listening to the still small voice of God, or listening to a trusted counselor challenge and exhort us, growth in wisdom will develop growth in proactive listening. Proactive listening will then, in turn, help us to answer well and consider carefully our communication with our spouse and others. Proactive listening will increase the pleasure and quality we find in our relationships.

Proverbs 18:13 states, "If one gives an answer before he hears, it is his folly and shame." Great advice! How often have you found yourself in the middle of an exchange with a friend, co-worker, or spouse, only to realize that they are not really listening? Usually, it's because they are too busy formulating their own response. Many times they don't even wait for you to finish your statement before they interrupt you to make their point. Although they may show the outward trappings of listening and considering your point of view, it is all too obvious that their thoughts and hearts are far from you.

But wait! Before we point the finger of accusation at others, how often have you found yourself in the middle of an exchange with a friend, co-worker, or spouse, only to realize that **you're** not really listening? Is it because you're too busy formulating **your own** response? Yep, we're just as guilty as those folks who bring such frustration into our lives. As always, change must begin with us!

Proverbs 18:13 speaks to the heart of the interrupter. Such a person is described as foolish and shameful. The frustration that the interrupter causes is boundless. Interrupting or forming your thoughts before you have heard the other view entirely is what causes communication to go sour and marriages to suffer. **We must learn to listen!**

Interrupting, or forming your thoughts before you have heard the other view entirely often causes miscommunication, misunderstanding, and mishandling of our most treasured relationships. **We must learn to listen!**

Interrupting, or forming your thoughts before you have heard the other view entirely is what causes quarrels, arguments, and wounded emotions. **We must learn to listen!**

Interrupting, or forming your thoughts before you have heard the other view entirely will cause those you love to lock you out of the communication process completely. **We must learn to listen!**

Listening carefully to everything your spouse has to say before forming your own response is a discipline that can be learned. But again, it won't happen by accident, and it won't happen without heart preparation. Those who become good listeners prepare themselves in advance to listen well. How do they accomplish this goal?

Good listeners prepare themselves in advance to slow down, stand still, and make eye contact.

A technique that has worked for us over the years is the intentional folding of our hands. When we need to listen to the communication of another person, and especially communication from one another, we discreetly fold our hands and make eye contact. These two simple, but intentional, disciplines force us to listen, and ultimately, to hear more completely. We have also learned to repeat a brief summary of what we just heard, back to one another. Doing this makes it clear that we are listening, and it also helps us slow down our responses.

As a helpful hint, repeating back a communication does not mean commentating on what was communicated. When we begin to commentate, analyze, and rearrange what was previously stated, we run the risk of miscommunication and misunderstanding.

Three tips for learning to listen:

1) Fold your hands discreetly

2) Make eye contact

3) Repeat a short summary back to the communicator

These three disciplines have produced so much fruit over the years. Not only do we "get it right" more often than we used to when we lacked the discipline to listen properly, but we now have a better marriage relationship as a result. The hard work involved was definitely worth the positive fruit in our marriage.

Let's be honest, we like people who listen to us, and we are frustrated by those who don't. Silence is not necessarily the same thing as listening. Silence is a powerful form of communication. In its best application, silence is a tool for increasing communication; however, used as a weapon, silence can break down and destroy bridges of communication. For more on the improper use of silence as a form of communication, see the last chapter titled, "Deal with Your Anger." Don't mistake controlling silence for proactive listening!

You can't make your spouse learn to listen, but you can discipline yourself to be a better listener. Learning to listen is one of the most important disciplines that any of us can possess. Successful marriages thrive on good communication. **Cracking the communication code starts when we learn to listen.**

RULE 2

FIND OUT THE FACTS...

"Facts are stubborn things; and whatever may be our wishes, our inclinations, or the dictates of our passion, they cannot alter the state of facts and evidence."

-John Adams

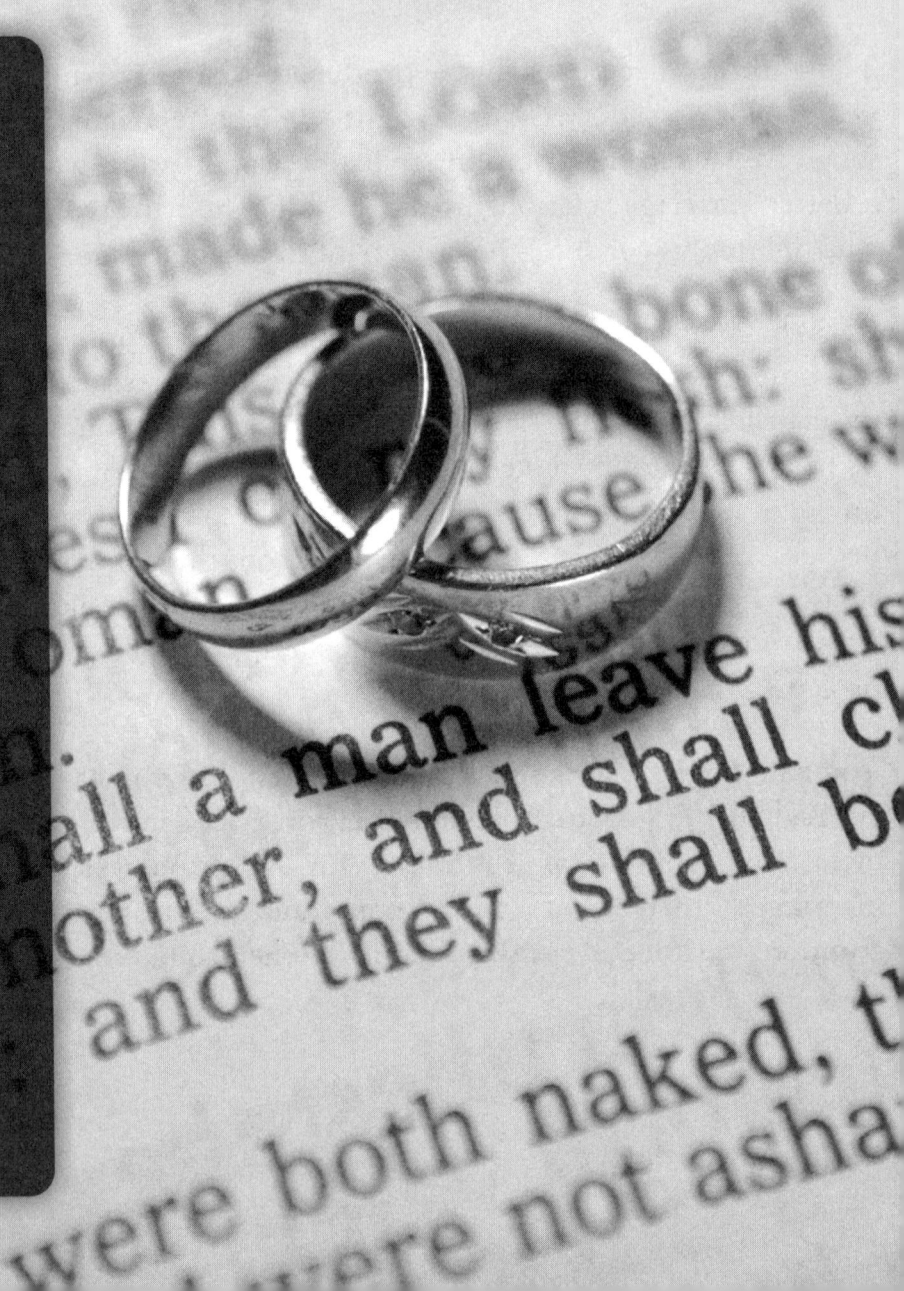

RULE 2

Find Out The Facts...

Expectations are nasty little things. Often, they creep up on us with no notice, and they can ruin our entire day. They can ruin our spouse's day. In fact, our expectations have the potential to ruin the day of anyone who inadvertently wanders into our path.

You might think of expectations as the snipers of good communication. Expectations take aim at good marriages and cause instantaneous pain. Most of us are completely unaware of our expectations for others until one of those expectations goes unmet. Then, look out!

Ugly, but persistent, our contentions wage war within us.

Don't confuse expectations with standards. Standards are developed through careful consideration. Standards are well established. Standards are clearly communicated. Standards help to build communication, solidify teamwork, and bring unity to a marriage and home. Standards build security instead of damaging the marital relationship.

Most couples play a little game with their expectations called the, "If you loved me, you would know" game. In this game, they build an expectation, which their spouse must then intuitively guess. Their unspoken assumption is that the other person will somehow read their mind and do exactly what is necessary to meet their unspoken expectation.

Most games are fun, but not this game. No, this game is different. Instead of explaining the rules before the game starts, we arbitrarily make up the rules as the game unfolds. Instead of beginning the game with equal playing pieces, this game stacks the deck. In the expectation game there is one winner and one very obvious loser. The expectation game stinks!

The 3 unwritten rules of the "Expectation" game are:

1) Never communicate (out loud) the expectation you are placing on the other person. They should just know… After all, if they loved you… they would know.

2) Become highly reactive and totally offended when your expectation isn't met. Remember, they should have known… After all, if they loved you… they would know.

3) Make sure the other person pays dearly for not meeting your felt need. Throw them under the bus as often as possible, so that next time they will work harder to meet your expectations… After all, if they loved you… they would know.

Sadly, the expectation game is played out millions of times each day in marriages all around the globe. Whether our spouse is eager to play or not, they are forced into participation in our poorly communicated expectation game. We have unspoken expectations for one another that go unfulfilled, and just like an unseen sniper, our unspoken expectations cause untold pain and suffering.

Often an individual who is married to someone with high expectations will be convinced that they are simply a "marriage failure." Because they seem to always miss the mark in meeting their spouse's unspoken expectations, they will begin to withdraw emotionally to avoid disappointing their spouse, inciting anger, and ultimately, failing once again. Want to cause distance in your marriage? Allow yourself to build expectations.

The immediate outcome of the expectation game is disappointment, discouragement, and anger. Although that's bad, the long-term outcomes of the expectation game produce even worse fruit. In the long run, marriages that are filled with continual expectations begin to wither. They don't end with a bang; instead the marriage relationship just begins to fizzle out as one partner emotionally withdraws from the "game."

What can you do to avoid the expectation assassins? **Find out the facts!**

The only person that we can change is us. You don't have the power to stop your spouse from having unrealistic and unspoken expectations for you; however, you can do something to eliminate your own uncommunicated and rather deadly expectations for them. In fact, not only **can** you make changes in the area of expectations, if you want a thriving marriage, you must **make** the necessary changes.

Find out the facts before you develop an expectation for your spouse.

Proverbs 13:10 says, "By expectations comes nothing but strife, but with those who take advice is wisdom." Great advice! Whenever you see strife or defensiveness as a result of your communication, you can rest assured that there is an unfulfilled expectation at the bottom of the discontent. The Proverb reminds us to take advice from others.

We're glad that you are here and paying attention. The first step to tearing down our expectation traps is recognizing their destructive nature and then seeking godly wisdom in order to recognize them. (Remember that wisdom back in Chapter 1? Now's the time to put your wisdom into action!) So, what can we do to avoid falling into the "expectation trap?" There are 3 actions you can take to avoid falling into the expectation trap in the future:

1) Ask Good Dialogue Questions.

The dialogue question is a great communication tool. The dialogue question allows you to communicate effectively while avoiding defensiveness. Consider the game show Jeopardy. Each statement by the contestants must be phrased in the form of a question. What, where, when, who, or how must precede each statement. As in Jeopardy, dialogue questions are non-accusatory questions. Notice that the term "Why?" is not included in the list of possible questions. "Why," by its very nature, is an accusatory word and implies guilt or premeditated action.

So, how does this work on a daily basis? Imagine you're a passenger in the car and your spouse is about to miss an important turn.

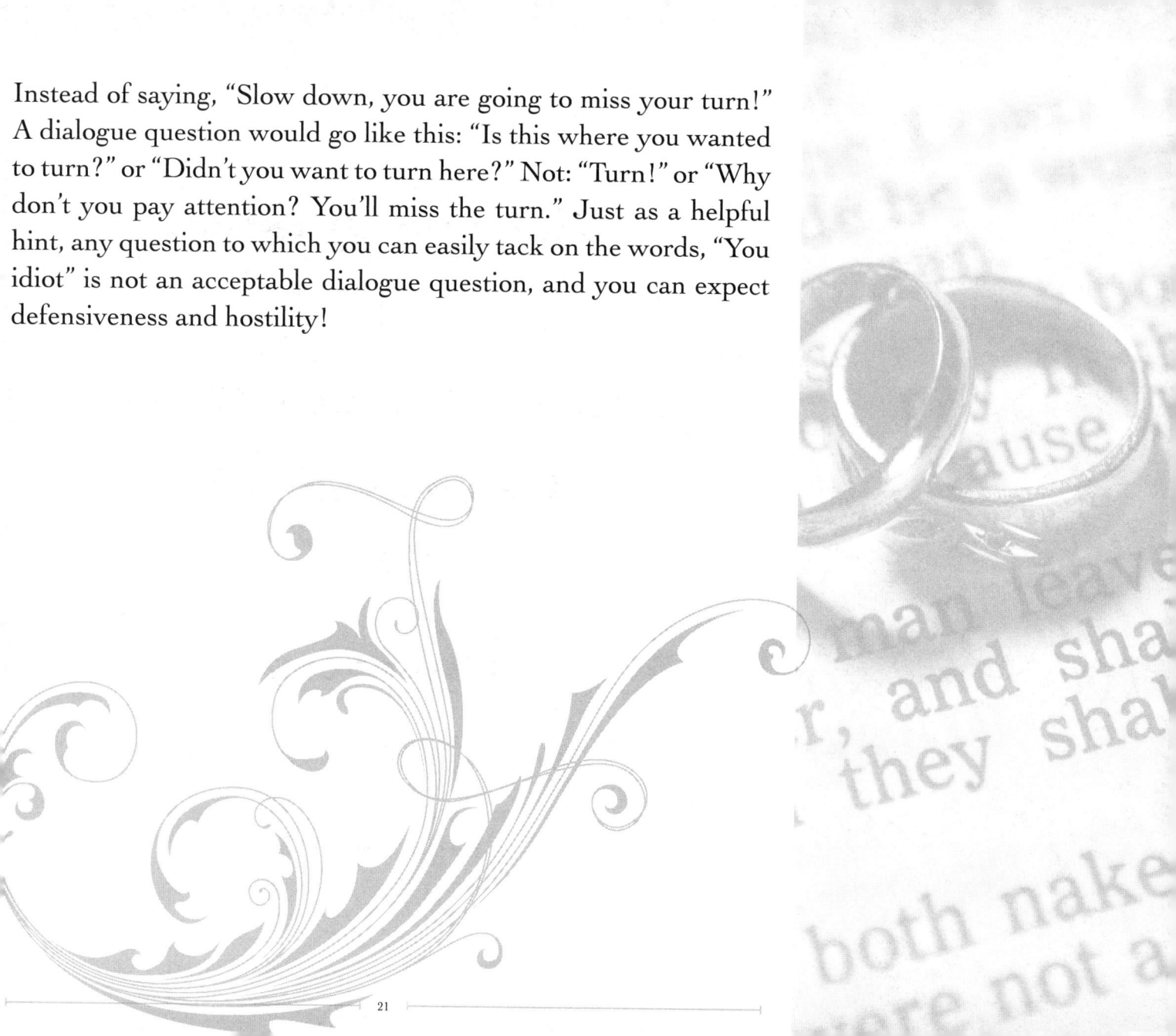

Instead of saying, "Slow down, you are going to miss your turn!" A dialogue question would go like this: "Is this where you wanted to turn?" or "Didn't you want to turn here?" Not: "Turn!" or "Why don't you pay attention? You'll miss the turn." Just as a helpful hint, any question to which you can easily tack on the words, "You idiot" is not an acceptable dialogue question, and you can expect defensiveness and hostility!

Dialogue Question

⬇

Data Gathering (Diffuse Defensiveness)

⬇

Discovery

⬇

Decision

The charm of the dialogue question is that it eliminates defensiveness by eliminating blunt accusation. We become defensive when others assign a motive to our behavior. We feel judged when someone accuses us, and we usually react defensively. To avoid such a reaction, simply phrase what you would like to communicate in the form of a question. This allows your spouse to make the desired discovery independently, and further, it then allows them to take ownership of that discovery.

When we take ownership of a discovery, we can then act on that discovery without feeling foolish or judged. Those actions that we take ownership of will become ingrained habits, causing change from the inside out. Harsh accusation or judgment may cause momentary change, but the heart will not be transformed. In fact, that momentary outward change may simply mask a wounded and discouraged heart.

Work dialogue questions into your vocabulary and watch the defensiveness in your marriage melt away.

Typical dialogue questions:

- Are you satisfied with how this job turned out?
- What is the speed limit on this stretch of road?
- Do you have the freedom to spend money on things for the house right now?
- I had planned to make dinner, but would you rather I sit and talk with you first?
- Can I help you with that, or would you rather do it alone?
- Can you think of a kinder way you could have asked me that question?
- What behavior do we expect while the babysitter is here?
- Could you have planned better?
- Are you saving any energy for me tonight? (hubba, hubba!)

2) Ask Yourself The Hard Questions

Examine your own motives before becoming offended by the actions of others. If you are the type of person who becomes easily offended or you find yourself in a perpetual state of strife, it is probably because you have a storehouse full of un-communicated expectations for others. The expectation trap is easy to fall into. You must learn to ask hard questions of yourself first before you become offended by your spouse's behavior.

Here's a simple truth about those hard questions of life: You must ask them of yourself. It is a rare friend that finds it comfortable to confront us with those hard questions. Stepping over the line of acceptability will unfortunately stop others from confronting us with the questions we so desperately need to hear regarding our actions and thought life. Don't put the onus for that responsibility on anyone else! Ask yourself those hard questions about your motives, and then develop an action plan to deal with what you discover about yourself. We are responsible to initiate change in our own lives; we can't foist that responsibility on to the shoulders of anyone else.

My marriage, parenting, and on-the-job relationships improved tremendously after I disciplined myself to stop playing the expectation game with others.

3) Today is the day to Make It Right!

Perhaps you are just **now** realizing that you have had expectations for your spouse and others. Possibly you now see the role your expectations have played in the strife around you. If so, now is the time to make things right with those whom you have offended. Make it a priority **today** to seek out those relationships that have been burdened by your expectations and ask them to forgive you. That's right... **Forgive you!** Use the words, "Will you please forgive me for my expectations?" Then, let them know how you intend to discipline your expectations in the future.

Let them know that in the future, you intend to find out the facts before you build an expectation.

> My marriage, parenting, and on-the-job relationships improved tremendously after I disciplined myself to stop playing the expectation game with others.

RULE 3

Think Before You Speak!

"Remember not only to say the right thing in the right place, but far more difficult still, to leave unsaid the wrong thing at the tempting moment."

-Benjamin Franklin

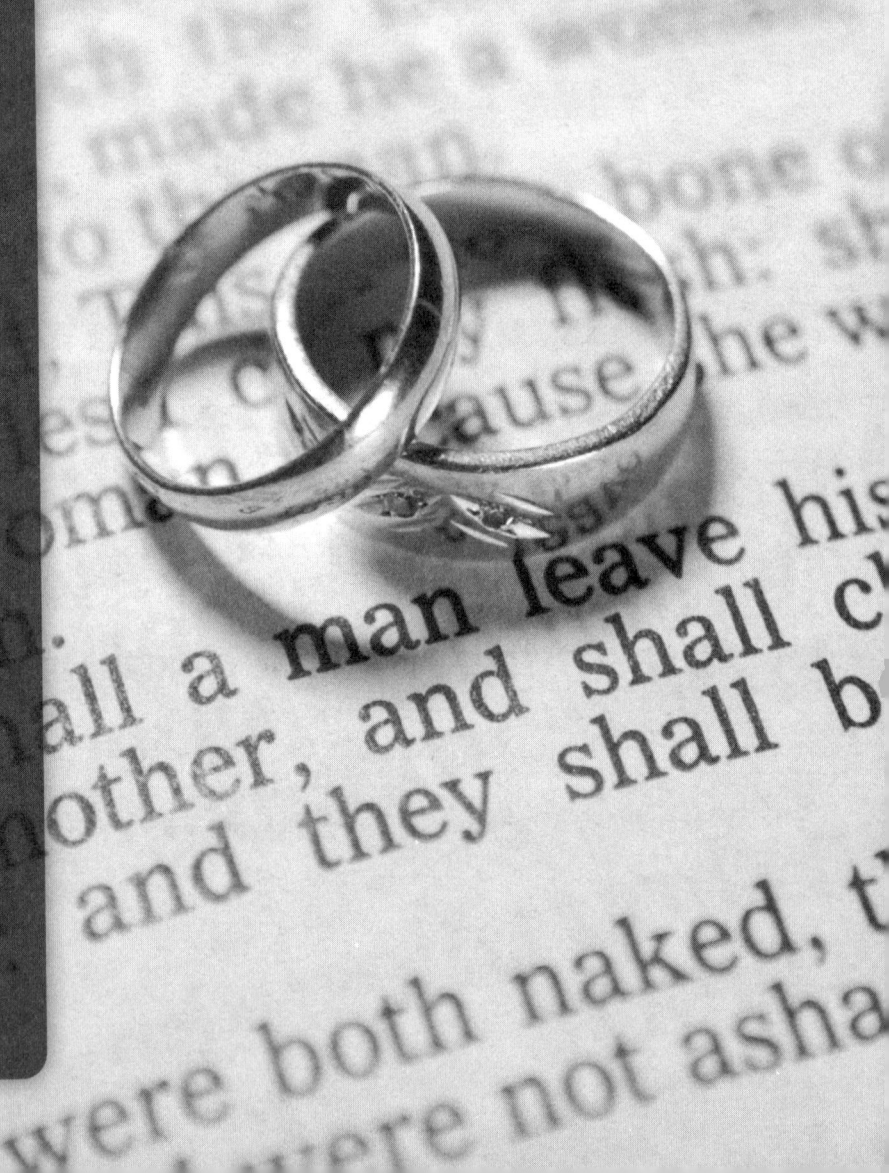

RULE 3

Think Before You Speak!

Can't you just hear your mother saying, "Why don't you think before you open your mouth?" We were notorious as kids for opening our mouths and inserting our foot. In fact, we're still pretty good at sticking our foot in our mouths at the worst possible moment. Unfortunately, sometimes we both manage that feat at the same time. That certainly makes for some interesting conversations!

How about you? Ever find yourself caught in an awkward situation because your lips started moving before your brain was engaged? The advice our parents gave us was wise. Think before you speak.

In marriage, it is critical to show wisdom in our speech. Often, our communication with our spouse becomes nothing more than a negotiation. If the negotiation doesn't go our way, we resort to pushing buttons to get what we want. We've both been known to raise our voice or give the silent treatment just to get what we want. Too often, we forget to think before we speak!

Many times (too many times) our mouths get us into trouble because we don't think before we speak.

I (Steve) have been employed at several different types of businesses over the years. I was a Senior Naval Officer for 29 years while I planted a church in northern New England and served as senior pastor of that ministry for 10 years. Since I have retired from both of those fields, I am now president of Characterhealth Corporation, a non-profit speaking, teaching, and corporate training organization. As well, I still fly the big airplanes for American Airlines.

Every job I've had brought unique challenges, but the one thing common to all of them was this… I needed to think before I spoke!

In the military, misplaced words can cause loss of life. Just ask the guys who languished in the Hanoi Hilton in Vietnam how they feel about Jane Fonda. As a pilot for AA, I must choose my words carefully because every word is recorded, and again, the wrong words in an emergency situation could lead to loss of life. I don't even want to tell you how hasty words can get you into trouble as a senior pastor… It's epic! **I needed to think before I spoke!**

For me, Megan, as a mom and ladies conference speaker, hastily spoken words can get me into hot water quickly. When I don't control the tone of voice I use with my children, my instruction becomes counter-productive. While my children may obey what I am saying, our relationship is damaged by my lack of concern for their precious hearts. Speaking without thinking in front of an audience of ladies can distort what I'm trying to teach. Sometimes, "being funny" robs my message of its clarity and purpose. At those times, I find myself doing more damage than good. **I need to think before I speak!**

Clearly, as the chief communicators for a company called Characterhealth, we'd both better be on our "A game" every day. There are those out there who are actively looking for Christians to say something that is questionable just so they can then pounce and attack. We don't need to give them any extra ammunition because of our careless speech. More importantly, we don't want to damage our personal testimonies or bring shame to the name of Christ because of our careless speech patterns.

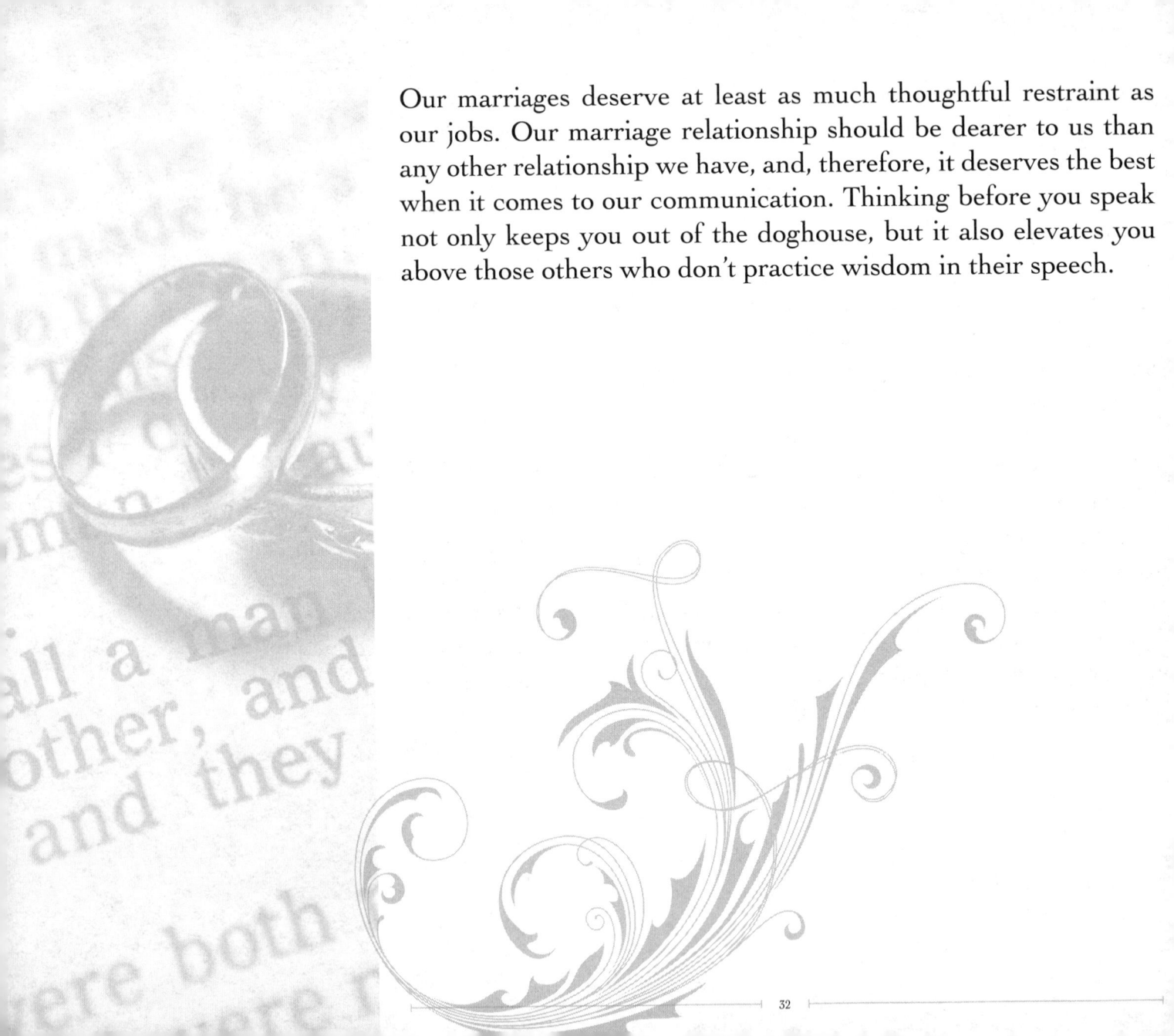

Our marriages deserve at least as much thoughtful restraint as our jobs. Our marriage relationship should be dearer to us than any other relationship we have, and, therefore, it deserves the best when it comes to our communication. Thinking before you speak not only keeps you out of the doghouse, but it also elevates you above those others who don't practice wisdom in their speech.

Proverbs 15:28 says it all: *"The heart of the righteous ponders how to answer, but the mouth of the wicked pours out evil things."*

Colossians 4:6 puts it this way: *"Let your speech always be seasoned with salt, so that you will know how you should respond to each person."*

At the end of the day, we can expect things to break, children to misbehave, and routines to be interrupted... That's all part of life around the house, and we don't have much control over the things that go wrong.

However, the one thing we do have some control over is what comes out of our mouths. We can choose our words carefully, and we can think before we speak. Three tips for developing wisdom in speech have been helpful to us over the years:

1) **Ponder!** Slow down and discipline yourself to say, "Can I think about that before I give you a response?" You don't want to ponder endlessly, but you do need to put some communication speed bumps up to slow yourself down, especially if you are inclined to speak before you think. Taking just a few moments to ponder before speaking can waylay the necessity of hours spent trying to undo the damage of thoughtless and hasty words.

2) **Learn from the example of others!** We have always enjoyed watching former Secretary of Defense Donald Rumsfeld answer a question. Often, after being asked a question from a reporter, he would stand behind the podium and just think. Sometimes it was a long time before he would respond, but it was certain that the responses he gave were well thought out. Learn from others that are older and wiser than you. Consider carefully what is being

asked or communicated, and then answer with an appropriately thought out response.

3) **Repeat back a short summary of what the other person said before you respond!** Good listening skills are essential for wise communication. We have trained ourselves over the years to repeat back a short summary of what we thought we just heard.

This discipline provides 3 benefits: 1) It lets your spouse know that you were listening to them. 2) It helps you get the facts straight before you respond. 3) It buys you some time to think before you speak!

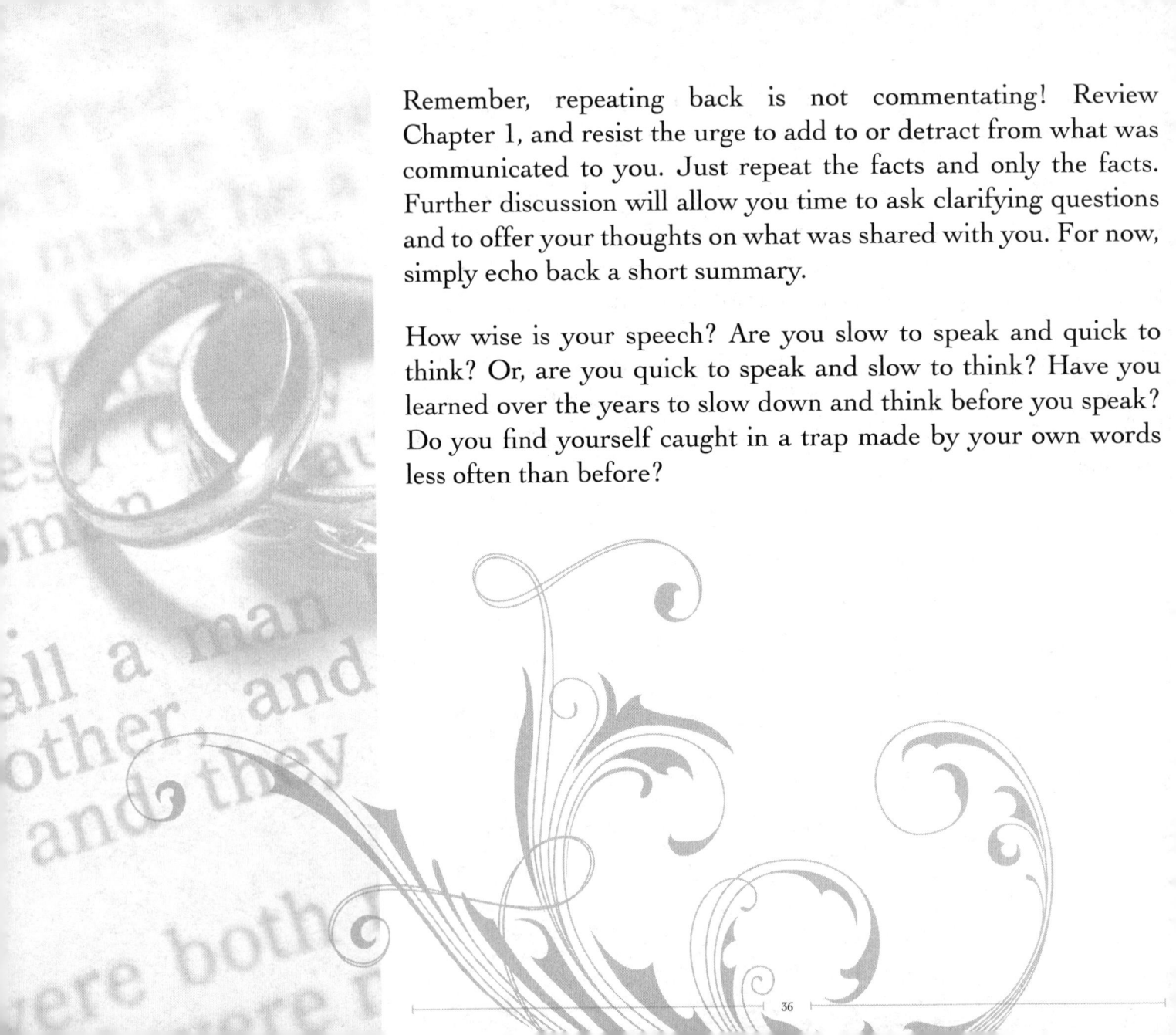

Remember, repeating back is not commentating! Review Chapter 1, and resist the urge to add to or detract from what was communicated to you. Just repeat the facts and only the facts. Further discussion will allow you time to ask clarifying questions and to offer your thoughts on what was shared with you. For now, simply echo back a short summary.

How wise is your speech? Are you slow to speak and quick to think? Or, are you quick to speak and slow to think? Have you learned over the years to slow down and think before you speak? Do you find yourself caught in a trap made by your own words less often than before?

> In our social media world, it is more important than ever to practice wisdom in our speech. The health of your marriage may just depend upon it!

RULE 4

Don't Get Defensive!

"What causes quarrels and what causes fights among you? Is it not this, that your passions are at war within you?"

-James 4:1

RULE 4

Don't Get Defensive!

How often have you found yourself in the middle of a quarrel over something that caught you completely off guard? Your spouse said something to you, then you responded poorly, then they retaliated, and pretty soon you're embroiled in one of those defensive moments that you wish you could avoid.... Don't we all?!

There are two reasons we respond to others defensively:

1) We are wrong! When we are in the wrong, we usually know it, yet we don't want anyone else to know it or point it out, especially our spouse. It is embarrassing. We naturally act defensively when they point out our error... **We all do!**

2) Our spouse assigns a motive to our behavior! They may be right about our motive, or they may be wrong. Regardless, we will always respond defensively when someone assigns a motive to our behavior. Why? We feel judged! When we feel judged we will defend ourselves instinctively... **You will too!**

So, what can we do to avoid defensiveness?

• **Let God be your defender!**

That's right… let God defend you. If you have nothing to hide, you should have nothing to be defensive about. A clear moral conscience is your best friend when it comes to avoiding defensiveness. As a bonus, God delights to defend us when we are choosing to honor Him with our life choices. Trust me, God can do a much better job of defending you than you could ever do!

We've learned two valuable practices over the years.

When we are wrong (and it is often…), we just own it. We don't make endless excuses.
We don't finger point and blame-assess. We just own it. It is very disarming to others when you say…

- Yep, that was me.
- I'm responsible for that blunder.
- It was my fault, and I will fix it.

If you are wrong, just own it. Don't rationalize the situation. Don't point the finger of blame elsewhere. Don't make excuses. **Just own it!**

In the process of owning our own bad behavior and wrong choices, it is easy to get caught in the, "Oh yeah? Well you _____." (We'll let you fill in the blank). If you were in the wrong, it makes no difference how the other person approached you, talked to you, or handled the situation. That's another issue altogether. Don't try to draw attention away from your own wrongdoing. No, instead learn to **own it!**

Sometimes, as spouses, we assign a motive to one another's behavior. Sometimes our children assign a motive to our behavior. We have trained ourselves to ask dialogue questions instead of becoming defensive. We usually ask questions like:

- Can you help me understand how you came to that conclusion?

- Are you sure you have all of the data or facts?

- Would you like to hear my side of the story?

- How can I help you understand my role in this issue?

If your spouse assigns a motive to your behavior, kindly and politely sidestep the issue, but whatever you do **don't go toe-to-toe with them**. Don't start a second conflict over the issue of an assigned motive. Instead, practice some of that long-suffering patience and just let that one go. If you get in the mix and begin to defend yourself, two things will happen. First, you'll only muddy the issue and prolong the conflict. Secondly, you won't be allowing God to be your defender. Remember, He can do a better job in your defense than you are able to do.

If you begin to defend yourself regarding the assigned motive, it will just end up making you look guilty. It also raises your blood pressure and does nothing to resolve the original issue at hand. You may win the argument but lose the battle, if you know what we mean. Now is the time to incorporate those well-practiced dialogue questions. Dialogue questions will help to side-step defensiveness, while at the same time collect data. That way, all parties involved can make an informed decision. Dialogue questions will also take you (personally) out of the line of fire. Now, God can be your defender.

Proverbs 24:29 puts it this way: *"Do not say, I will do to him as he has done to me. I will pay the man back for what he has done."*

The example of the Greatest Communicator of all time is important to note. Jesus never reviled others, even when he was being reviled. Jesus was never in the wrong. Jesus never needed to admit wrongdoing. He was quick to diffuse the situation and to allow His Father to come to His defense. 1 Peter 2:23 says, "When He was reviled, He did not revile in return; when He suffered, He did not threaten, but continued entrusting Himself to Him who judges justly."

Jesus continually let God be his defender.

How about you? Are you confident enough to let God defend you? It may be instinctive to want to defend ourselves, but it is far better to step back, take a deep breath, and let God do the defending for us.

Wise husbands and wives ask good questions. Also, they let their good work speak for itself, and they rarely get tangled up in petty defensive arguments.

Don't feel the need to defend yourself. After all, you have a great Defender already. Let Him speak on your behalf. Like the good heavenly Father that He is, God is eager to defend His children

RULE 5

CONSIDER ONE ANOTHER'S SPIRIT

A little Consideration, a little Thought for Others, makes all the difference.

-Winnie the Pooh
Pooh's Little Instruction Book

RULE 5

Consider One Another's Spirit

I (Steve) just read an article in Time magazine titled, "The Me, Me, Me Generation" by Joel Stein. The subtitle of the article is "Millennials are lazy, entitled narcissists who still live with their parents… why they'll save us all."

I read this article with great interest. I found it to be very well written and balanced with humor, conjecture, and solid research. In fact, I loved this story so much, that I devoted two hours of my seminary class on discipleship to reading and discussing the article. The takeaway thoughts from Mr. Stein were many and varied.

According to the author, Millennials, a group made up mostly of teens and 20-somethings, are narcissistic, overconfident, lazy folks. They build their relationships via social media. They crave instant access, and they are constantly holding up cameras and cell phones to take pictures of themselves. Those ubiquitous self-photos are called "selfies." My teenagers are relentlessly clicking them, and then posting them to Facebook for comments from their friends.

Interestingly, according to Stein, this generation will "save us all."

Stein goes on to explain that the Millennials are not a rebellious generation. They have nothing to rebel against, since they are the first generation to grow up without an establishment. He describes them as lazy and entitled. They are willing to stay at home and delay marriage. Much like Peter Pan in the timeless story by J.M. Barrie, this generation doesn't want to grow up, and their parents are subsidizing their Neverland.

This generation will most likely be the first American generation to earn less money than their parents. We believe the Millennials are the direct result of the Dr. Spock permissive parenting model that was introduced in the 1960's. The "I'm OK, you're OK" mindset of the American culture has produced fruit, and that fruit is the "Me, Me, Me, generation."

So what?! What's the big deal about looking out for #1? What harm do "selfies" cause, even though they may be rather obnoxious? In the long run, Millennials are harmless… or are they?

When you are constantly looking out for yourself, you do so at the expense of others.

Regardless of what the myriad of post-modern, self-esteem gurus teach, self-centeredness does not make for a good marriage.

A good husband or wife must be focused on meeting the needs of the other. They consider what is good for their spouse before they think about themselves. Character healthy spouses are counterintuitive. They often swim against the current. They defy conventional wisdom, and that's what makes their marriages so successful.

Character healthy spouses are "big picture" lookers. They consider the long-term relational ramifications of their decisions, and they base their choices on what will be best for the marriage "team." They are willing to give up their perceived rights for the sake of unity and oneness.

Character healthy spouses don't keep a record of "who got what, when". Instead, they rejoice in the success of their spouse. They are happy when their spouse receives a special blessing. They certainly don't play the tit-for-tat game of "You owe me!" Character healthy spouses have happy, although imperfect, marriage relationships.

At the heart of a winsome marriage is the drive to focus on the needs of others first.

Jim Collins described such behavior in his New York Times bestselling book, Good to Great. Collins calls these effective people "Level 5 Leaders." Level 5 leaders are humble, unassuming, and always looking out for the well-being of those that work for them, and in the case of marriage, with them.

Good communicators get the most out of relationships because people love working for humble, unassuming folks who keep the best interests of others in mind. Good marriages thrive when each spouse keeps the best interests of the other in mind. A good marriage demonstrates the principle of putting the other guy first in the finest possible manner.

Good marriages are winsome to those who witness them. These are the marriages that make you wonder what they are doing differently. We can tell you for certain that these marriages aren't just "lucky." No, to have such a marriage takes work, commitment, and an ability to subvert your own desires for the well-being of your spouse.

Proverbs 18:19 states, *"A brother offended is harder to be won than a strong city, and contentions are like the bars of a citadel."*

Unlike the Me, Me, Me culture of 21st century America, character-healthy marriages march to the beat of a different drummer. Consider the other guy first? Always! Spouses who put themselves last are amazingly successful. They do not cause offense in action, word, or deed. They do, in fact, create an atmosphere of goodwill that produces relational dividends for years to come. In fact, we have found in our own marriage that those relational dividends far outweigh any "thing" we might have sacrificed for the good of one another.

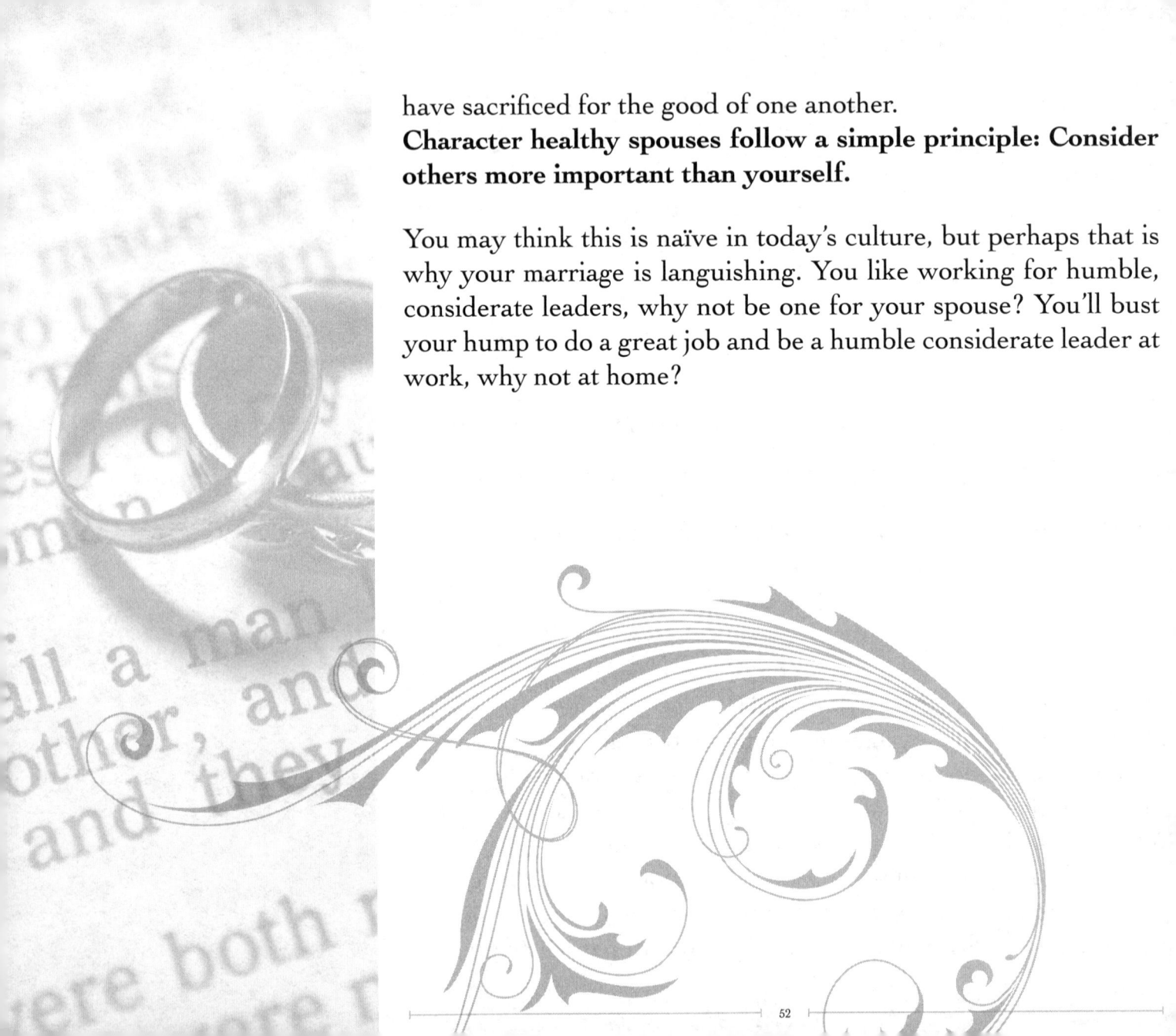

Character healthy spouses follow a simple principle: Consider others more important than yourself.

You may think this is naïve in today's culture, but perhaps that is why your marriage is languishing. You like working for humble, considerate leaders, why not be one for your spouse? You'll bust your hump to do a great job and be a humble considerate leader at work, why not at home?

What type of *marriage* do you want?

It may come down to what type of spouse you're willing to be!

Me, me, me...

Or

You, you, you?

Think about it!

RULE 6

GUARD YOUR TONGUE

If anyone thinks he is religious and does not bridle his tongue but deceives his heart, this person's religion is worthless.

-James 1:26

RULE 6

Guard Your Tongue

The tongue is such a small part of the body, yet it gets us into some pretty big trouble. In Chapter Three of James' New Testament Epistle he writes, "So also the tongue is a small part of the body, and yet it boasts of great things." His description of the power of words is very accurate. James goes on to describe the tongue as a restless evil that sets our lives on fire.

Words can be used for good, but all too often they are used to tear down, discourage, and slander, especially those closest to us.

Therefore, we must learn to guard our tongues. Once the words are spoken, it is impossible to get them back. We were watching the news this morning where Paula Deen, the famous (now former) Food Network cook, was apologizing for using racial slurs at her restaurants. Too little, too late!

Once the words are out, the damage is done, the pain is inflicted, and the clean-up operation must commence.

Guarding your tongue is one of the most important relationship disciplines you will ever possess. How many famous (and not so famous) people have been dethroned, dropped, or otherwise canned, because of ill-advised and poorly chosen words? You would think that people in the public eye would know how to guard their tongue, but many don't. Closer to home, how many marriages have ended in divorce, or worse, due to the exchange of harsh words? As Christians, we should know better: however, the Christian track record is no better than the secular when it comes to divorce and dysfunction.

The cost of cleaning up the mess our words cause is immense.

Our words are so powerful, that one misplaced word can ruin a marriage, poison our children, and terminate our employment.

So, how do you guard your tongue? How do you avoid falling into the "wrong word at the wrong time" trap that so many others have fallen into over the years? How do you transform a restless evil into a reliable resource?

Proverbs 15:1-4 provides some good counsel in this regard: *"A gentle answer turns away wrath, but a harsh word stirs up anger. The tongue of the wise makes knowledge acceptable, but the mouth of fools spouts folly. The eyes of the Lord are in every place, watching the evil and the good. A soothing tongue is a tree of life, but perversion in it crushes the spirit."*

We learn 3 important disciplines for the tongue from this passage:

1) **Gentle words are always a good idea.** Stirring the pot with harsh words is rarely a good idea. Our harsh words usually come back to bite us. You may get the short-term response you want by using harsh words, but it will be at a long-term cost. It's easy to start the fire, but putting out the fire may prove difficult, if not impossible.

Choose words that will diffuse rather than ignite.

2) **Learn to Listen.** *(See Chapter 1)* The fool is the one who does not listen well. By contrast, the wise man learns to listen. Whereas the fool is always spouting off, the wise among us make knowledge acceptable. Trust me, you want to be the type of person that your spouse wants to hear from and approach for counsel and comfort; however, if you talk without ceasing or spout off with every complaint that passes through your mind, you will eventually say something you regret and your marriage may not recover. We all know a couple where one of the pair runs at the mouth. If you are constantly talking, you are not listening. The simple truth is that most of us just want someone to listen. The best thing you can do for your marriage is learn to listen!

The wise among us make knowledge acceptable.

3) ***Avoid Perversion***. The old saying, "You are what you eat" is not only true regarding the intake of food; it is also true regarding the intake of spiritual influences. Examine closely the music you listen to. Is it full of harsh lyrics and ugly words? What do you watch on TV? Where do you go on the Internet? We must have great discernment when it comes to our character development. One thing is true regarding the proper care and feeding of our spirit… Garbage in, garbage out!

It may be permissible to feed on perverse content, but is it profitable?

Guarding the tongue is more than just choosing your words carefully. Guarding the tongue starts with the discipline of closely monitoring what we watch, listen to, and expose ourselves to on a recurring basis. If we realize that any of those inputs are causing us to speak without putting a guard over our tongue, then they must go! Sometimes, choosing to honor God and our spouse by carefully tending to our tongue will require radical amputation of whatever is hindering that process.

Is there anything you are reluctant to discard in order to elevate your standard of communication?

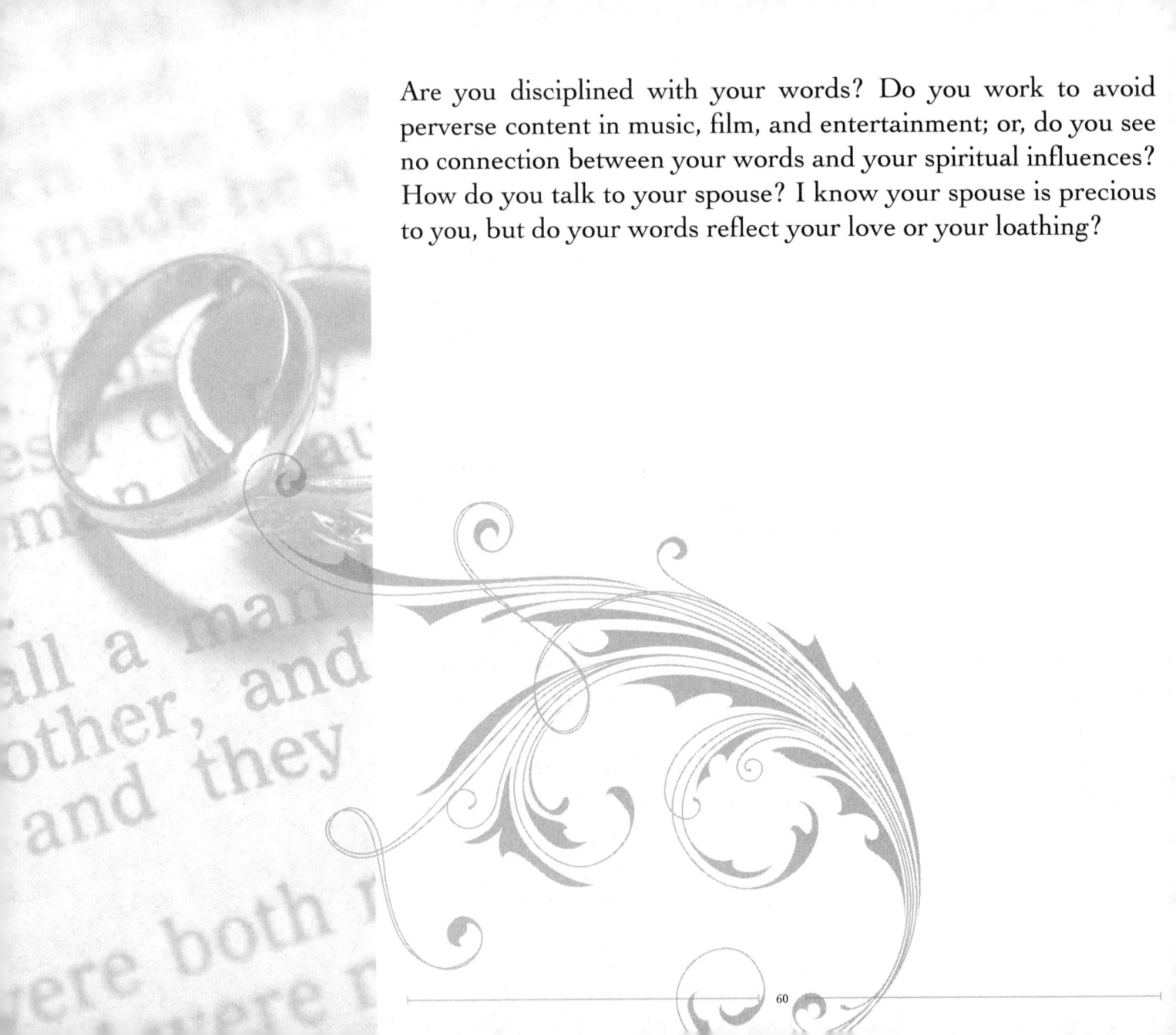

Are you disciplined with your words? Do you work to avoid perverse content in music, film, and entertainment; or, do you see no connection between your words and your spiritual influences? How do you talk to your spouse? I know your spouse is precious to you, but do your words reflect your love or your loathing?

The discipline to guard your tongue may be the single most valuable relationship-building tool you will ever possess.

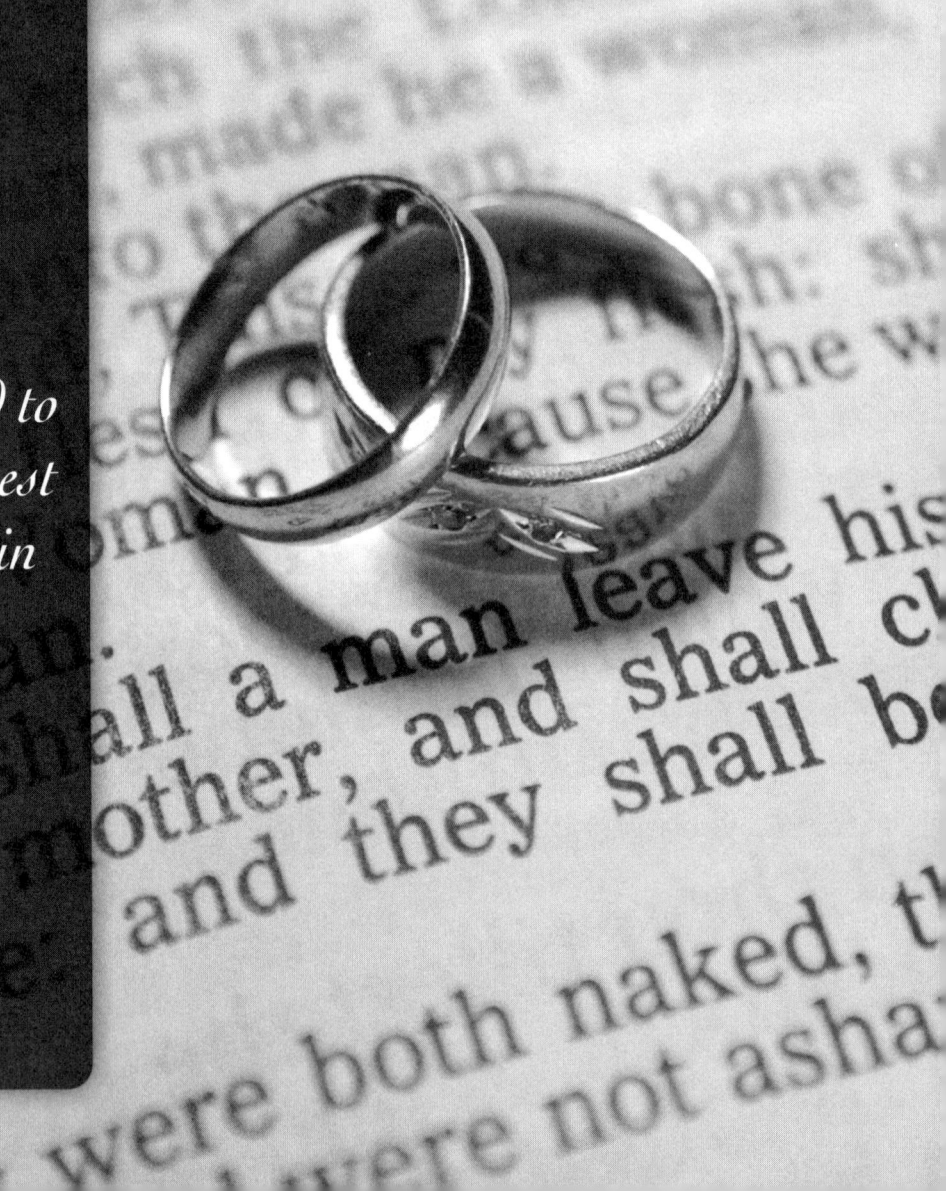

RULE 7

RAISE THE STANDARD

Let us raise a standard to which the wise and honest can repair; the rest is in the hands of God.

-George Washington

RULE 7

Raise the Standards

Just because everybody else seems to be cranky and irritable these days doesn't mean you should be as well! Imagine your mother saying, "Just because your friends are doing it, doesn't mean you should do it too."

People tend to be a lot like sheep. We follow the crowd. We tend to act like those around us with little regard for the impact of our choices. If you run with a highly "reactive" crowd, you will tend to be reactive yourself. On the other hand, if you run with a highly "proactive" crowd, you will tend to put on proactivity as a way of life.

Successful marriages resist drifting with the crowd.

Husbands and wives must deliberately and consistently raise the standard of communication.

How do you raise your personal standard of communication?

By getting plugged into something bigger than yourself!

For some of us, raising the standard of personal communication means we communicate to please God. Our choice of words and tone are chosen to please God and to satisfy His higher standard.

For others, raising the standard means keeping the bottom line in mind. Harsh words, short tempers, cranky tones, and filthy language are bad for marriages. Just because our culture is becoming loose in terms of vulgar speech doesn't mean it is a good idea for your marriage or your family.

Husbands and wives must deliberately and consistently raise the standard of communication.

Colossians 4:6 says, *"Let your speech always be with grace, as though seasoned with salt, so that you will know how you should respond to each person."*

Speech seasoned with grace is not phony or insincere; rather, it is speech that is considerate and appropriate given the context of the situation. Speech seasoned with grace will heal, rather than wound. It will build, rather than destroy. Speech seasoned with grace is delicious, delightful, and demonstrative of the grace of God.

1 Peter 3:8-10 describes what it looks like to raise our communication standards:

"To sum up, all of you be harmonious, sympathetic, brotherly, kindhearted, and humble in spirit; not returning evil for evil or insult for insult, but giving a blessing instead; for you were called for the very purpose that you might inherit a blessing. For the one who desires life, to love and see good days, must keep his tongue from evil and his lips from speaking deceit."

Raising the standard in communication requires 3 actions:

1) **Season your speech with salt.** Choose to be gracious and kind before you are faced with a reason not to be gracious or kind. The proactive communicator plans in advance to be considerate and self-controlled when faced with a potentially heated discussion.

If you are in the habit of allowing yourself to "speak your mind" just in your thoughts, it won't be long until those angry words come spilling out. Choosing to be gracious and kind ahead of time requires us to control what goes on in our thoughts just as diligently as we control what comes out of our mouths. You can only hide what is happening on the inside for a limited time, so take the necessary steps to discipline and subordinate your thoughts.

Good communicators don't get rattled because they have planned ahead for success.

2) **Be God's Instrument.** Effective communicators are plugged into something bigger than themselves. They don't allow themselves to take things personally. They restrain their words because they want to make God look great. The most successful marriages do not return insult for insult. Husband and wife are always thinking about something bigger than themselves, especially if that "something" is their marriage.

In the spirit of I Corinthians 13, good communicators are always hoping and assuming the best. Instead of continually wondering, "What did he/she mean by that?" They take what is said at face value and discipline themselves not to assign a motive or go down a road that was not intended.

Time to raise the standard… The health of your marriage may just depend upon it.

They don't allow themselves to take things personally.

3) **Tell The Truth.** Once you gain a reputation as a liar, It is hard to shed that label. Effective communicators tell the truth, regardless of the personal cost to them. Telling the truth, for them, is more important than the short-term benefit that may come as a result of a quick lie to cover face; however, telling the truth doesn't mean you have to be harsh or blunt. You can tell the truth in love, with respect for the other person's feelings.

How truthful are you? Do you exaggerate to make yourself look better? Are you quick to own up to your mistakes, or are you prone to make up a story to cover up your mistakes? Are you a finger pointer or a blame assessor?

Once you have gained the reputation for being untruthful, it will be almost impossible to change that reputation. Even when you speak the truth, others will wonder if it is the whole, accurate, unembellished truth. We must work intentionally to gain and retain a testimony of truthfulness and accuracy in our speech.

Remember, it's never the crime that does you in; it is always the cover up!

RULE 8

DEAL WITH ANGER

My dear brothers, take note of this: Everyone should be quick to listen, slow to speak, and slow to become angry, for man's anger does not bring about the righteous life that God desires"

-James 1:19-20

RULE 8

Deal With Anger

It is shocking how many of us consider anger to be the one-size-fits-all emotion when it comes to dealing with conflict or disappointment. When our expectations aren't met, we reach for the angry response and put everyone around us on edge. Even on a good day, our normal response is edgy, irritable, and argumentative.

If your spouse acts like they are walking on eggshells around you, it is probably because you habitually respond to them with anger.

The ancient Greeks identified three types of anger:

1) ***Perorgismos:*** This is a low level of mild irritation; the type of anger a mother of toddlers runs around with all the time. We call this type of anger ***baseline anger.*** We mistakenly believe that we can live with this low level of baseline anger. In fact, at times it seems virtuous to just maintain the status quo and not rock the boat. However, over time, those who don't deal with the troublesome issues in their marriage, workplace, or with their children, will steadily raise the baseline level of irritation until it suddenly overflows into a full-blown fight.

Perorgismos is insidious.

2) ***Orge:*** This form of anger is best thought of as indignation. For example, you have been waiting your turn in line at the airport to speak with the gate agent, when someone else cuts in front of you to ask a "quick" question. You respond with ***Orge... indignation.*** You may even confront the stranger with angry words of rebuke for their rude inconsideration. You feel as though you had a right and that right was taken from you.

Orge often accompanies an injustice.

3) ***Thumos:*** This is **explosive anger.** Loss of control is associated with . You may become so angry that you throw something or hit something or someone out of rage and total frustration. **Thumos** may begin as a slow boil and come to eruption, or it may show itself as a quick flash of violent and explosive anger.

Thumos is very visible and can be life-threatening.

Ephesians 4:26 is a familiar Bible passage that has been repeated often throughout the years, and for good reason. It states: *"Be angry yet do not sin, do not let the sun go down on your anger."*

This verse reminds us of how important it is to deal with our anger in its infancy, well before things escalate out of control. In fact, the Greek word used here in Ephesians 4:26 is the word Perorgismos, not Orge or Thumos, as you might think.

The instruction to us all is to deal with our anger while it is still in the stage of mild irritation. If we deliberately confront the situation and resolve the issue while it is still in this irritation phase, whatever it is will never reach the indignation or out-of-control phase. Great advice indeed.

So, who are you?

Are you the Perorgismos type? Do you walk around with a low level of irritation all the time? Have you convinced yourself that's just the way life is, and you're going to have to live with it? How awful! You don't have to live in a perpetual state of irritation.

Are you the Orge type? Are you always indignant about something? Perhaps you listen to too much talk radio or you are party to too much gossip. Cynicism and gossip feed our indignation, and ultimately, raise our blood pressure. Turn the dial and walk away from the gossip. You will be glad you did.

Are you the Thumos type? Do you lose it from time to time? Do you scare yourself sometimes? Get help! Schedule an appointment to see your pastor. Seek counsel. Do something before you hurt yourself or someone dear to you.

Deal with your anger now, before you lose your marriage and your family. Anger is not the one-size-fits-all emotion. It is much better to deal with your anger now, than to have someone else deal with it for you later.

Discipline yourself to aim your angry energy at the problem not the person!

The waitress did not overcook your steak. If you want to get it resolved, talk to the manager or talk to the cook, but don't shoot the messenger. Did your children leave their bikes out in the rain? That's their bad not your wife's fault. Too often, we lash out at those closest to us, simply because they are accessible. Deal with your anger before your anger deals your marriage a fatal blow.

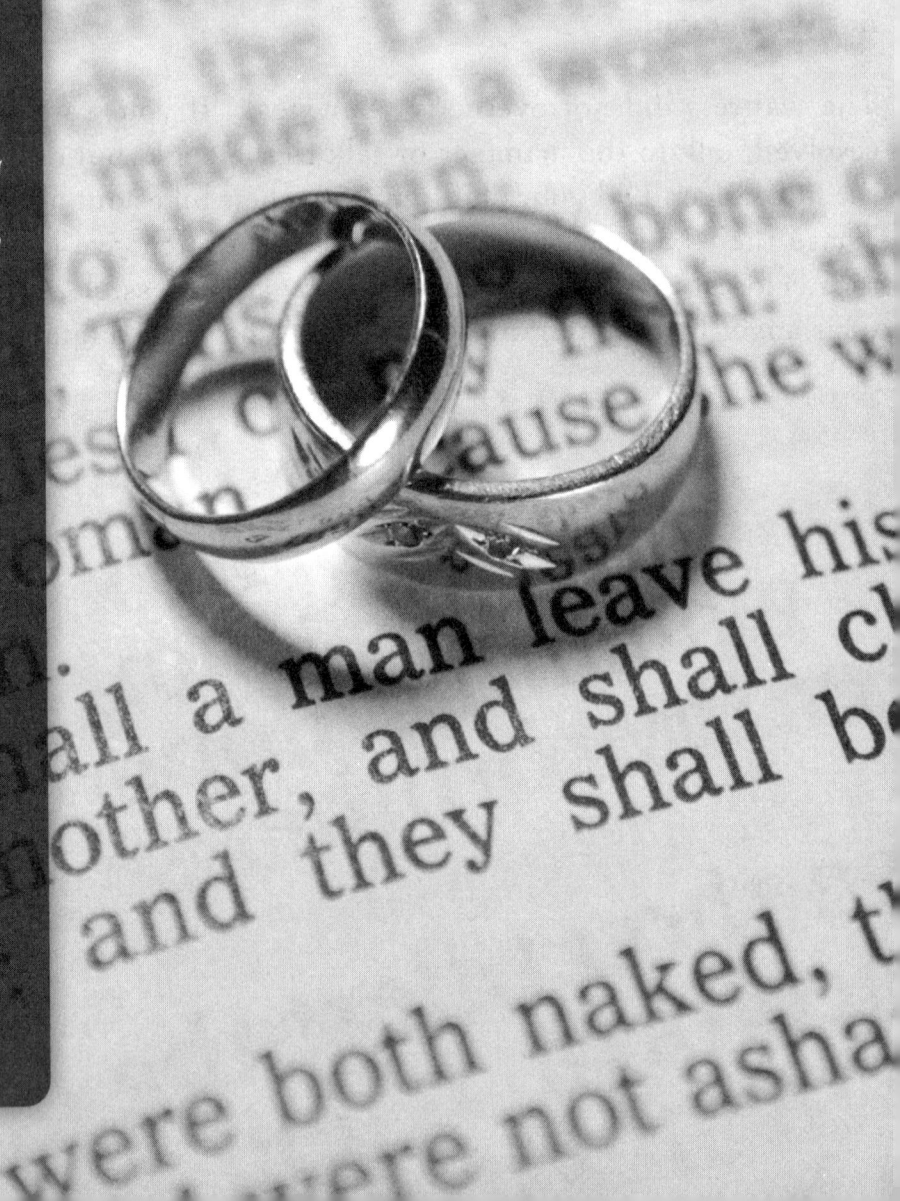

CONCLUSION

Success in marriage does not come merely through finding the right mate, but through being the right mate.

~Barnett R. Brickner

CONCLUSION

We all get it. We know the textbook answer. Good communication is absolutely vital to a growing and thriving marital relationship. Good communication can help rebuild a struggling marriage, continue the growth of a good marriage, and elevate a good marriage to a great and God-honoring marriage.

Now, are you ready to get beyond the textbook? Are you ready to put in the hard work necessary to move your marriage to that high, but attainable, level of a great and God-honoring marriage?

You have the tools. Now it's your turn to put them to work.

Learn to listen. Slow down and really seek to understand what your spouse is sharing with you. Build the habit of listening before you speak.

Find out the facts. Do whatever it takes to stop the no-win expectation game in your marriage. Take the steps necessary to right the wrongs that your own out of place expectations have caused.

Think before you speak. Take just a few moments to consider what was said and then respond with appropriate and relationship-building communication. Train yourself to be slow to speak and quick to think…not vice versa.

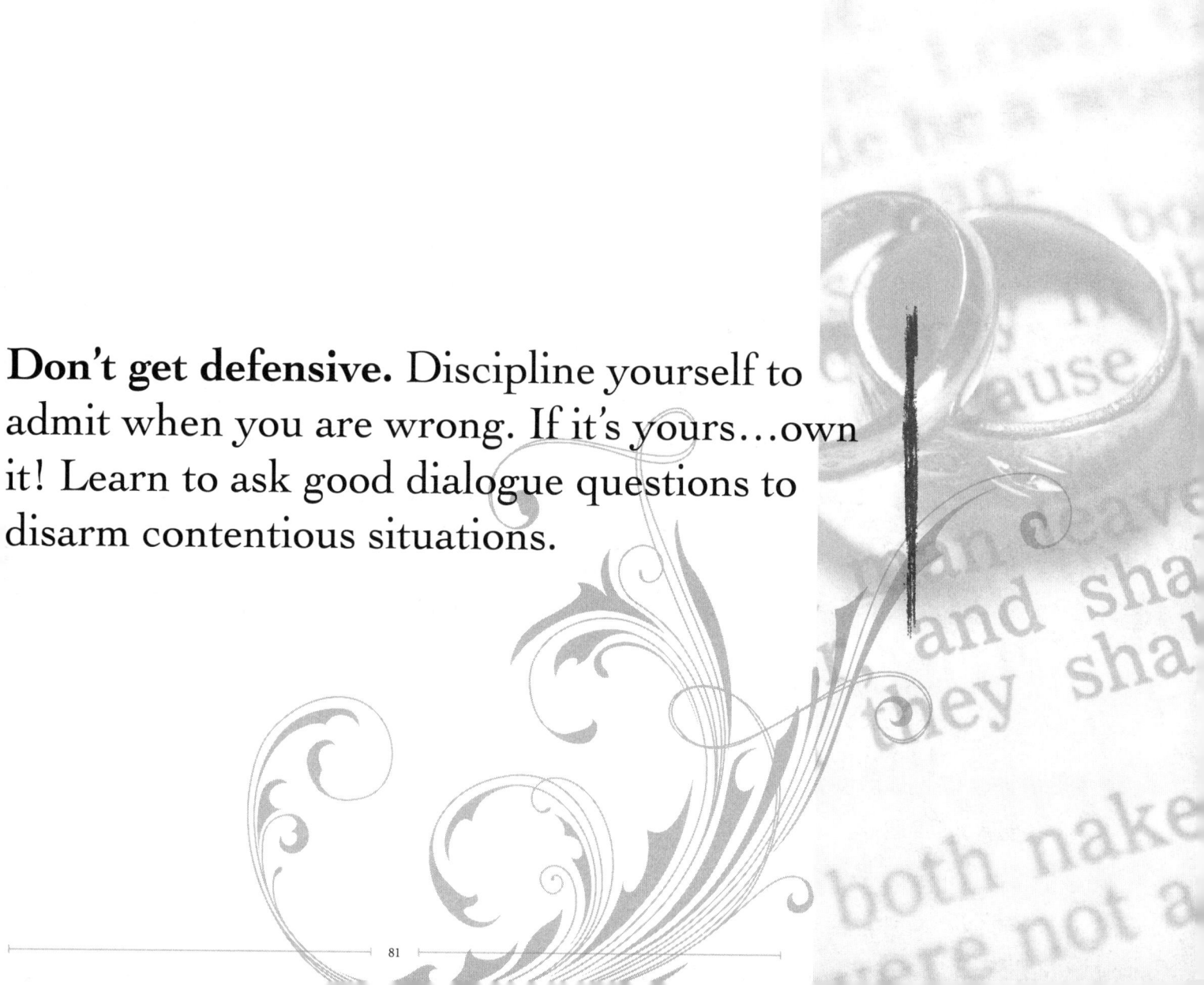

Don't get defensive. Discipline yourself to admit when you are wrong. If it's yours…own it! Learn to ask good dialogue questions to disarm contentious situations.

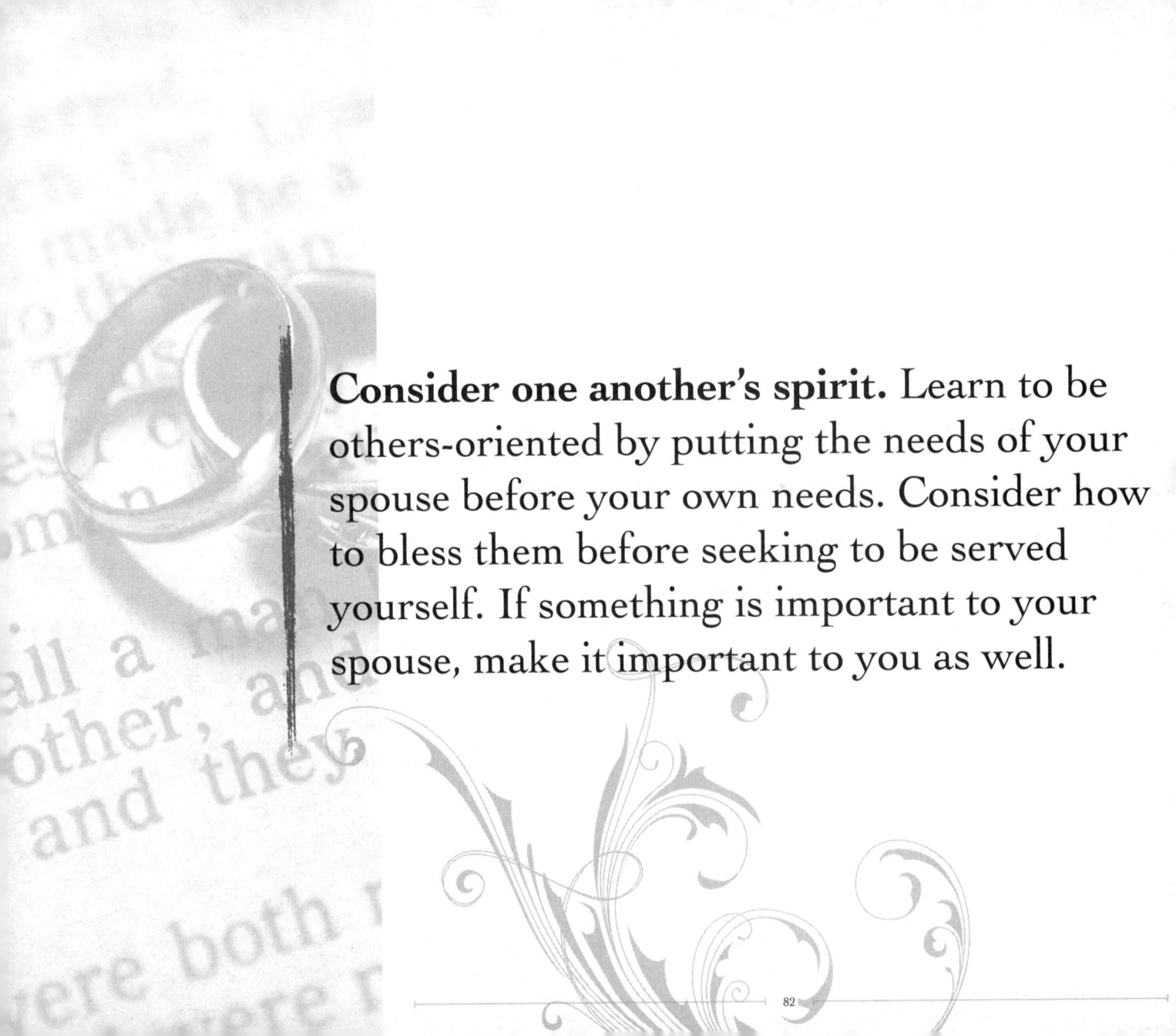

Consider one another's spirit. Learn to be others-oriented by putting the needs of your spouse before your own needs. Consider how to bless them before seeking to be served yourself. If something is important to your spouse, make it important to you as well.

Guard your tongue. Remember, words spoken in haste will take an inordinate amount of time to resolve. Fill you heart with good and uplifting resources in order to build a basis of proactive and positive words as the overflow of your heart.

Raise the standard. It doesn't matter what anyone else's marriage looks like; your marriage should bring honor to God. Speak with grace. Speak with truth. And, most importantly, be God's instrument of blessing in the life of your spouse.

Deal with anger. Regardless of what type of anger you struggle with, take the necessary steps to subordinate your anger to the Word of God. Replace anger with understanding and outbursts with gentleness. Build peace in your marriage through your tender responses to conflict.

Learning to communicate effectively will increase the pleasure you find in your marriage. It will dramatically increase your testimony to others. Most importantly, it will show a watching world what a marriage, committed to honoring God, looks like on a daily basis.

We're praying for you as you learn to communicate successfully!

Steve and Megan

RESOURCES

Other Books by Megan Ann Scheibner:

In My Seat: A Pilot's Story from Sept. 10th–11th

Grand Slam: An Athletes Guide to Success in Life

Rise and Shine: Reciipes and Routines For Your Morning

Lunch and Literature

Dinner and Discipleship Studies in Character

The A-Z Guide to Character Healthy Homeschooling

Other Books by Steve Scheibner:

Bible Basics

Books by Steve and Megan Scheibner:

Character Matters: A Daily Step-by-Step Guide to Developing Courageous Character

Studies in Character

The King of Thing and the Kingdom of Thingdom

DVD Series Available:

Parenting Matters: The Nine Practices of the Pro-Active Parent

Marriage Matters: Create the Joy-Filled Marriage of Your Dreams

Character Matters: The Nine Practices of Character Healthy Youth

Subscribe to Seve and Megan's blogs:

www.SteveScheibner.com   www.MeganScheibner.com

You can find these books and other resources at:

CharacterHealth.com